978 1648 334184
AF400961

JESUS
IS
LOVE

Help us God each day,
To follow you along the way.
Teach us to be kind like you,
In everything we say and do.
Amen

Jesus loves the little children
All the children of the world
Morning, noon, and every night
They are precious in His sight
Jesus loves the little children
of the world.

HE IS RISEN

JESUS LOVES YOU